tiny
yarn
animals

Amigurumi Friends
to Make and Enjoy

Tamie Snow

Photography by Nich...

HOME

A HOME BOOK
Published by the Penguin Group
Penguin Group (USA) Inc.
375 Hudson Street, New York, New York 10014, USA
Penguin Group (Canada), 90 Eglinton Avenue East, Suite 700, Toronto, Ontario M4P 2Y3, Canada (a division of Pearson Penguin Canada Inc.) • Penguin Books Ltd., 80 Strand, London WC2R 0RL, England • Penguin Group Ireland, 25 St. Stephen's Green, Dublin 2, Ireland (a division of Penguin Books Ltd.) • Penguin Group (Australia), 250 Camberwell Road, Camberwell, Victoria 3124, Australia (a division of Pearson Australia Group Pty. Ltd.) • Penguin Books India Pvt. Ltd., 11 Community Centre, Panchsheel Park, New Delhi— 110 017, India • Penguin Group (NZ), 67 Apollo Drive, Rosedale, North Shore 0632, New Zealand (a division of Pearson New Zealand Ltd.) • Penguin Books (South Africa) (Pty.) Ltd., 24 Sturdee Avenue, Rosebank, Johannesburg 2196, South Africa

Penguin Books Ltd., Registered Offices: 80 Strand, London WC2R 0RL, England

While the author has made every effort to provide accurate telephone numbers and Internet addresses at the time of publication, neither the publisher nor the author assumes any responsibility for errors, or for changes that occur after publication. Further, the publisher does not have any control over and does not assume any responsibility for author or third-party websites or their content.

Copyright © 2008 by Tamie Snow
Cover art by Boli Graphics
Cover design by Nicholas Noyes
Text design by Pauline Neuwirth, Neuwirth & Associates, Inc.

First edition: August 2008

Library of Congress Cataloging-in-Publication Data

Snow, Tamie.
  Tiny yarn animals : amigurumi friends to make and enjoy / Tamie Snow ; photography by Nicholas Noyes.—1st ed.
    p. cm.
  Includes index.
  ISBN 978-1-55788-530-2
  1. Crocheting—Patterns. 2. Soft toy making. I. Title.
  TT829.S67 2008
  745.592'4—dc22   2008013935

PRINTED IN MEXICO

10 9 8 7 6 5 4 3 2 1

Most Home books are available at special quantity discounts for bulk purchases for sales promotions, premiums, fund-raising, or educational use. Special books, or book excerpts, can also be created to fit specific needs.
For details, write: Special Markets, Penguin Group (USA) Inc., 375 Hudson Street, New York, New York 10014.

Introduction

I make dolls.
I make them because they are adorable. I make them because they make terrific gifts. But I mostly make them because I can't stop! After your first doll, I guarantee, you'll be hooked, too (no pun intended).

I'm Tamie Snow, the designer behind Roxycraft.com. I started Roxycraft in 2003 as a free pattern website of my original crochet and knit patterns. Mostly they were of bags, scarves, and hats with a smattering of craft project tutorials for things like marble magnets and record bowls.

I started crocheting Amigurumi-style dolls in the summer of 2005. I had a belly full of my son, Jackson, and really wanted to make some toys for him to hold in his teeny tiny hands. Who knew there would be so many people who wanted to make little dolls, too? Not me. It's been a wonderful surprise!

Amigurumi...What?
If you dabble in the online crochet world, no doubt you have seen this word by now. It's been all the rage in the forums for a couple years.

But if not, here's a short lesson.

Amigurumi translated from Japanese is "stuffed toy." Obvious, no? But there is more to it. It's a style of crochet, born in Japan, focusing on the cute factor . . . think Sanrio. The first ones I ever saw were large-headed animals with wide, low-set eyes and very small arms and legs. They are generally made by crocheting in a spiral without joining at the end of a round like you would with a granny square or a doily.

How to Get Started
Are you ready to make some dolls? Let me impart some of the knowledge I've stumbled upon along the way. (But before we begin, grab a 4.0mm crochet hook, some inexpensive acrylic yarn, and let's get started.)

Your Basic Stitches
If you're completely new to the world of crochet, use these basic stitches and techniques to create the tiny yarn animals you see in this book. For more crocheting instruction, check out the resources section on page 60.

MAKING A SLIPKNOT AND YARN OVER

Make a loop over your middle and pointer fingers, pull a loop through it from behind, and tighten down leaving a hole for your hook.

Insert the hook into the hole and tighten the knot to the hook.

Make sure the working end (the end attached to the skein) is hanging behind your hook. Pull the working end over the hook toward you to create a yarn over.

MAKING A CHAIN

Make a slipknot, insert the hook into the loop, yarn over (a), and draw loop through loop on the hook (b). Continue to create a chain (c).

SLIP STITCH

In Amigurumi, the slip stitch is used most often to join loops to form a ring. Insert hook in stitch (a), yarn over (b), and draw through loop on hook (c).

SINGLE CROCHET

Insert hook in a stitch (a), yarn over (b), and draw loop through the stitch and through loop on hook (c).

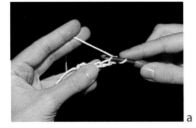

HALF DOUBLE CROCHET

Yarn over (a), insert hook in stitch (b), draw loop through, yarn over (c), and draw through all three loops on hook (d).

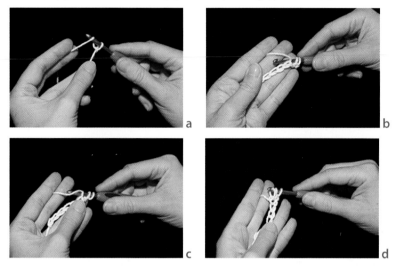

DOUBLE CROCHET

Yarn over (a), insert hook in the next stitch (b). Yarn over (c), and pull yarn through stitch (d). Yarn over (e), and pull yarn through two loops on hook (f). Yarn over (g), and pull yarn through last two loops on hook (h).

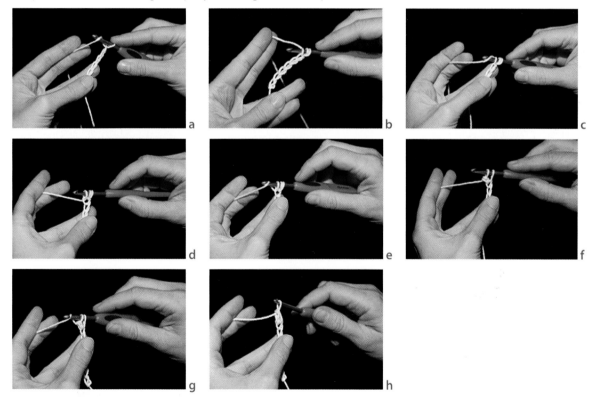

TREBLE CROCHET

Yarn over twice (a), insert hook in stitch indicated (b), yarn over, and pull up a loop, then yarn over and draw through two loops on hook (c). Yarn over (d), and pull up a loop again (e). Yarn over (f), and pull up a loop for a third time (g).

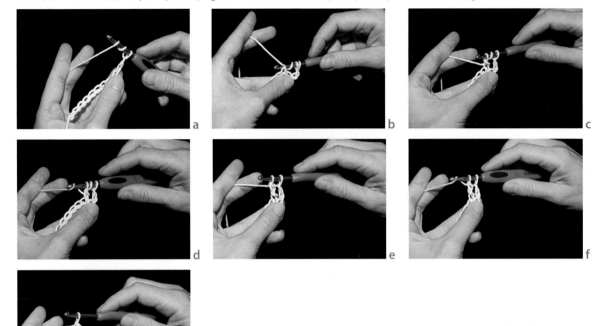

WHERE ARE THE BACK LOOPS?

Every stitch has two loops on the top. Most of the time, you insert your hook under both loops. The loop closest to you is the front loop and the one farther away is the back loop. Working in the back or front loops can create a decorative effect or, in the case of Amigurumi, can help make bends in the fabric for sharper corners.

PICOT

A picot gives a delicate decorative edge to crochet pieces. It is performed in this book using these instructions: chain 3, insert hook in the 1st chain, yarn over, and draw through all remaining loops on hook.

Assembling Your Tiny Yarn Animal

Now that you've learned the stitches, it's time to make your first doll. Let's get started.

How Do I Put a Doll Together?

After you have crocheted all the pieces according to the instructions (I will have some assembly directions in the pattern themselves), it's time to sew the pieces together . . .

What you'll need is an embroidery needle large enough for yarn and some patience. If you've never attempted using a needle and thread before, this may be intimidating at first. The nice thing about working with yarn is that it all sort of blends in and, with practice, you'll be a whiz in no time.

Basically, you need to know the whip stitch, which is explained simply as the "in-and-out stitch." You stick the needle in one crocheted piece and pull it out the next, and repeat.

When joining two open ends, it'll be obvious where you should stitch (where the stuffing is visible). But, when you attach an open piece (say, an arm or a foot) to a closed piece (like the side of the body) it might be more daunting. Just pick up stitches as you go and you'll do fine.

Finishing Details

To put a face on your doll you will need embroidery floss and a sharp embroidery needle. You will be using basic stitches to add eyes, a nose, and sometimes a little smile to your doll.

If you aren't very comfortable using a needle and thread, there are other techniques, such as fabric paint, buttons, doll eyes, "puff paint," and much more. I encourage you to express your own creativity!

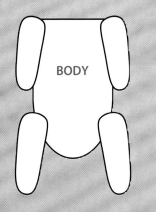

BODY

How to Read the Patterns

From experience, I know that someone new to crochet can be a little confused about pattern reading. It all just sounds like nonsense until you know what you're reading.

For example, what is the gauge? 2 stitches x 2.5 rows = 1" Uh, what? Math? A little, yes. Gauge is a way to make sure that the piece you are making is going to come out looking like the one in the picture. Whipping up a 5" x 5" swatch and counting the stitches and rows will save you a lot of time and energy in the long run.

When making a doll, the gauge is just a guideline for size. If your doll is a little bigger or smaller, it won't be the end of the world. But if you're making a sweater, the gauge is extremely important.

As a rule, I generally try to leave out as many abbreviations as I can simply because I think it's easier for my readers to understand, especially the newbies! I mean, who wants to have a cheat sheet in hand the whole time?

ABBREVIATIONS USED IN THIS BOOK

ch = chain

sc = single crochet

hdc = half double crochet

dc = double crochet

tr = treble crochet

sc2tog = single crochet two stitches together

mm = move marker

FO = finish off

The term "finish off" usually refers to creating one chain, cutting the yarn, and pulling the tail through to secure your work from coming undone. For this book I suggest leaving a 6" to 9" tail of yarn to use when stitching the pieces of the dolls together. Use your embroidery needle to weave in your ends.

Tips for Making Your Tiny Yarn Animals

Making these dolls involved a great deal of trial and error on my part. I would like to save you the time and give you the lowdown on what I've picked up over the years.

Use the Cheap Stuff

I love, no, *adore* expensive yarn. It feels incredible in my hands and makes my projects looks amazing.

So what's with all the inexpensive yarn used in this book? In my experience, it's the best for making dolls. It's durable, washable, and holds its shape beautifully. I promise I won't hold it against you if you decide to spring for the fancy stuff . . . I get it, I do. In fact, I feature a couple of my dolls in this book made with the pricier stuff. For more on what the dolls in this book are made of, see page 61.

Think About Texture and Gauge

Though gauge is not important for dolls in general, a few of the patterns in this book provide a specific gauge for reference. If you want the dolls you're making to look exactly like the dolls in this book, I suggest you check your gauge and use the recommended materials. Otherwise the end result may look different in size and shape.

To Join or Not to Join

There is a bit of debate on whether using a join at the end of your rounds still qualifies the doll as Amigurumi. Let me add my two pennies . . .

I used to crochet dolls with a join, and I have done it without, and in my experience the difference is minimal. The downside to using a join is the seam (which is easy to disguise with proper stuffing), and the downside to spirals is the stitch markers (which can be a pain). Pick your poison.

As to whether it is truly Amigurumi or not . . . a cute doll is the goal, right? So join 'em if you want to, I say.

Do It Tight, Do It Right

OK, this might be going against everything you experienced yarn artists have been taught about loose even stitches, but I'll ask you to please just forget all you know! If you're a beginner, you're in luck—no habits to break!

When making the animals, keep your stitches even but make them tight! Not so tight that you can't get your hook in on the next round, but you should definitely be tightening it down with a gentle tug after each stitch.

Stay on the Right Side

This is something I've noticed on the Internet—lots of people turn the poor little dollies inside out! I know that both sides look very similar, but the patterns are written to make a right-side-out doll. An inside-out doll will be lumpier and that's because it's fighting its own shape.

Stuff It Silly

Polyester fluffy stuffing is cheap, so don't scrimp . . . SPLURGE. Stuff that doll until you can't get any more stuffing in there!

The best method for stuffing is small bits at a time. A pinch of fluff in every stuff . . . OK, now I am getting carried away. But seriously, you should patiently stuff your doll a small bit at a time and stuff it to death. I promise you'll see a difference!

And don't be afraid to mold it. Once the doll is assembled, you may still see lumps. Just rub 'em out! Roll it, squish it, punch it—it can take it.

A fun addition to the stuffing is weighted polyester (poly) beads (found in the same section as the stuffing material in your local craft store). They give a realistic weight to your doll and can help with keeping it right-side up for display purposes.

I keep my poly beads in an old water bottle for easy pouring. Fill up your doll's body, stuff the beads down, and fill it again. Take a small amount of the fluffy polyester stuffing material and stuff it in the top to hold the beads in place.

tiny **yarn** animals

Lamb, page 30

Pig, page 32

Lion, page 34

Elephant, page 36

Frog, page 37

Beaver, page 38

Koala, page 40

Hippo, page 41

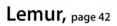

Lemur, page 42

Bumblebee, page 44

Owl, page 46

Pup, page 45

Bear, page 48

Penguin, page 50

Turtle, page 52

Hedgehog, page 56

Octopus, page 57

Lamb

MATERIALS

4.0mm crochet hook

Worsted weight yarn in off-white and gray

Embroidery floss in pink

6mm black safety doll eyes, beads, or buttons

Polyester stuffing material

Polyester beads for stuffing

Embroidery needle

GAUGE

24 stitches x 24 rows = 4"

FINISHED SIZE

Approx. 4"

Head

With off-white

R1–ch2, 6sc in 2nd chain from hook, mm

R2–2sc in each sc around (12sc), mm

R3–*2sc in 1st sc, 1sc in next, repeat from * around, mm

R4–*2sc in 1st sc, 1sc in next 2sc, repeat from * around, mm

R5–*2sc in 1st sc, 1sc in next 3sc, repeat from * around, mm

R6 thru R10–sc in each stitch around, mm

R11–*sc2tog, 1sc in next 3sc, repeat from * around, mm

R12–*sc2tog, 1sc in next 2sc, repeat from * around, mm

On this doll, the face is at the top of the ball, where the spiral began and the back of the head is where you closed the hole.

Attach eyes wide-set and midway down the face.

R13–*sc2tog, 1sc in next sc, repeat from * around, FO

Stuff firmly.

R14–sc2tog in each stitch around, FO

Set aside.

Body

With off-white

R1–ch2, 6sc in 2nd chain from hook, mm

R2–2sc in each sc around (12sc), mm

R3–*2sc in 1st sc, 1sc in next, repeat from * around, mm

R4 thru 7–sc in each stitch around, FO

R8–*sc2tog, 1sc in next 4sc, repeat from * around 3 times total, mm

R9 thru 11–sc in each stitch around, FO

Stuff with poly beads.

Attach head to body using whip stitch.

Arms and Legs (make 4)

With gray

R1–ch2, 6sc in 2nd chain from hook, mm

R2 thru 6–sc in each stitch around, FO

No need to stuff the arms and legs.

Use tail to stitch up the tiny hole where you finished off. You should be left with a little appendage that looks like a sausage.

For the legs, stitch to the sides of the body section near the bottom (not to the bottom of the body).

For the arms, stitch into the crux of the neck.

Refer to the chart on page 5 for placement of appendages.

Ears (make 2)

With off-white

R1–ch2, 6sc in 2nd chain from hook, mm

R2–sc in each stitch around, mm

R3–*2sc in 1st sc, 1sc in next, repeat from * around, mm

R4 thru 6–sc in each stitch around, FO

Sew ears to head.

Placement of the ears is key! You want the ears to be
attached to the lower sides of the head pointing south.

Snout

With gray

R1–ch2, 6sc in 2nd chain from hook, mm

R2–2sc in each sc around (12sc), mm

R3–sc in each stitch around, FO

Attach the snout right between the eyes, not below!

Using pink embroidery floss or 2 strands of pink yarn,
stitch nose and mouth onto snout.

Pig

MATERIALS

4.0mm crochet hook

Worsted weight yarn in pink

6mm black safety doll eyes, beads, or buttons

Polyester stuffing material

Polyester beads for stuffing

Embroidery needle

GAUGE

24 stitches x 24 rows = 4"

FINISHED SIZE

Approx. 4"

Head

R1–ch2, 6sc in 2nd chain from hook, mm

R2–2sc in each sc around (12sc), mm

R3–*2sc in 1st sc, 1sc in next, repeat from * around, mm

R4–*2sc in 1st sc, 1sc in next 2sc, repeat from * around, mm

R5–*2sc in 1st sc, 1sc in next 3sc, repeat from * around, mm

R6 thru R10–sc in each stitch around, mm

R11–*sc2tog, 1sc in next 3sc, repeat from * around, mm

R12–*sc2tog, 1sc in next 2sc, repeat from * around, mm

On this doll, the face is at the top of the ball, where the spiral began, and the back of the head is where you closed the hole.

Attach eyes wide-set and midway down the face.

R13–*sc2tog, 1sc in next sc, repeat from * around, FO

Stuff firmly.

R14–sc2tog in each stitch around, FO

Set aside.

Body

R1–ch2, 6sc in 2nd chain from hook, mm

R2–2sc in each sc around (12sc), mm

R3–*2sc in 1st sc, 1sc in next, repeat from * around, mm

R4 thru 7–sc in each stitch around, FO

R8–*sc2tog, 1sc in next 4sc, repeat from * around 3 times total, mm

R9 thru 11–sc in each stitch around, FO

Stuff body with poly beads.

Attach head to body using whip stitch.

Arms and Legs (make 4)

R1–ch2, 6sc in 2nd chain from hook, mm

R2 thru 6–sc in each stitch around, FO

No need to stuff the arms and legs.

Use tail to stitch up the tiny hole where you finished off. You should be left with a little appendage that looks like a sausage.

For the legs, stitch to the sides of the body section near the bottom (not to the bottom of the body).

For the arms, stitch into the crux of the neck.

Snout

R1–ch3, 1sc in 2nd chain from hook, 4sc in next sc, 3sc in underside of the 2nd chain again, join with slip stitch to form ring (8sc total)

R2–in back loops only, sc in each stitch around, FO

To attach, sew snout in between eyes, slightly above them.

Ears (make 2)

R1–ch2, 6sc in 2nd chain from hook, mm

R2–sc in each stitch around, mm

R3–*2sc in 1st sc, 1sc in next, repeat from * around, mm

R4–sc in each stitch around, FO

Place ears on the top sides of the head—not right on the top and not parallel to the eyes, but between those points.

Lion

MATERIALS

4.0mm crochet hook

Worsted weight yarn in yellow and hot pink

Embroidery floss in black and white

Polyester stuffing material

Polyester beads for stuffing

Embroidery needle

GAUGE

24 stitches x 24 rows = 4"

FINISHED SIZE

Approx. 4.5"

Head

With yellow

R1–ch2, 6sc in 2nd chain from hook, mm

R2–2sc in each sc around (12sc), mm

R3–*2sc in 1st sc, 1sc in next, repeat from * around, mm

R4–*2sc in 1st sc, 1sc in next 2sc, repeat from * around, mm

R5–*2sc in 1st sc, 1sc in next 3sc, repeat from * around, mm

R6–*2sc in 1st sc, 1sc in next 4sc, repeat from * around, mm

R7 thru R13–sc in each stitch around, mm

R14–*sc2tog, 1sc in next 4sc, repeat from * around, mm

R15–*sc2tog, 1sc in next 3sc, repeat from * around, mm

R16–*sc2tog, 1sc in next 2sc, repeat from * around, mm

R17–*sc2tog, 1sc in next sc, repeat from * around, FO

Stuff firmly.

Set aside.

Body

With yellow

R1–ch2, 6sc in 2nd chain from hook, mm

R2–2sc in each sc around (12sc), mm

R3–*2sc in 1st sc, 1sc in next, repeat from * around, mm

R4 thru 13–sc in each stitch around, FO

Stuff body with poly beads.

Attach head to body using whip stitch.

Arms and Legs (make 4)

With hot pink

R1–ch2, 6sc in 2nd chain from hook, mm

R2 thru 6–sc in each stitch around, FO

No need to stuff the arms and legs.

Use tail to stitch up the tiny hole where you finished off. You should be left with a little appendage that looks like a sausage.

For the legs, stitch to the sides of the body section near the bottom (not to the bottom of the body).

For the arms, stitch into the crux of the neck.

Refer to the chart on page 5 for placement of appendages.

Mane

With hot pink

Pick up stitches around the head to create a base row.

You do this by inserting the tip of your hook under an existing stitch, yarn over, draw up a loop, and sc. Continue doing this until you have a row of sc. The number of stitches doesn't matter but try to space them evenly (no clumping).

Once the base row is complete:

ch1, turn, *sc in 1st stitch, ch3, sc in same stitch to form picot, repeat from * across to last stitch

You should have 1 picot for every stitch in your base row. In the photo, there are 19.

Use ends to secure the mane to the head.

Face Embroidery

You will be embroidering with floss and hot pink yarn. The yarn is 4-ply, which means it's made up of 4 strands of thin yarn wound together to make a stronger whole. You will need to know how to separate those strands for both the embroidery floss and the yarn.

Nose

With 2 strands of hot pink yarn, stitch an upside-down triangle in the center of the face.

In the photo, the triangle covers 2 rows and is 4 stitches wide at the widest point.

Eyes

With 3 strands of black embroidery floss, stitch a shallow oval that is 1 row high and 3 stitches across at the widest point.

At the outer corner of each eye, stitch on 3 eyelashes (think crow's feet).

With 3 strands of white, add a small sparkle to each eye in the outer corner.

Mouth

With 3 strands of black embroidery floss, stitch a short straight line down 2 rows long for the tip of the nose, then backstitch a slightly upturned smile that spans 6 rows.

Stitch a little open mouth in a *U* shape.

Elephant

MATERIALS

5.0mm crochet hook

Worsted weight yarn in hot pink

6mm black safety doll eyes, beads, or buttons

Polyester stuffing material

Embroidery needle

GAUGE

Varies

FINISHED SIZE

Approx. 3–5"

Body

R1–ch2, 6sc in 2nd chain from hook, mm

R2–2sc in each sc around (12sc), mm

R3–*2sc in 1st sc, 1sc in next sc, repeat from * around, mm

R4–in back loops only, sc in each stitch around, mm

R5 thru 11–sc in each stitch around, mm

R12–*sc2tog, 1sc, repeat from * around, FO

Stuff.

Head

R1–ch2, 6sc in 2nd chain from hook, mm

R2–2sc in each sc around (12sc), mm

R3–*2sc in 1st sc, 1sc in next, repeat from * around, mm

R4–*2sc in 1st sc, 1sc in next 2sc, repeat from * around, mm

R5–*2sc in 1st sc, 1sc in next 3sc, repeat from * around, mm

R6 thru 10–sc in each sc around, mm

R11–*sc2tog, 1sc in next 3sc, repeat from * around, mm

R12–*sc2tog, 1sc in next 2sc, repeat from * around, mm

Attach eyes wide-set and midway down the face.

R13–*sc2tog, 1sc in next sc, repeat from * around, mm

Stuff.

R14–sc2tog around, FO

> *If you're using snap-on doll eyes, remember to have them in place before stuffing or assembly.*

Ears (make 2)

ch2, 3sc in 1st chain from hook, ch1, turn

2sc in each sc, ch1, turn

2sc in each sc, ch1, turn

2sc in each sc, FO

Arms (make 4)

Working in rounds

R1–ch2, 4sc in 1st chain from hook, mm

R2–2sc in each sc around, mm

R3–working in back loops, sc around, mm

R4 thru 6–sc around, FO

Stuff.

Trunk

Working in rounds

R1–ch2, 5sc in 1st chain from hook, mm

R2–working in back loops, sc around, mm

R3 thru 12–sc around, FO

Finishing

Assemble doll as shown in picture.

Weave in ends.

Frog

MATERIALS

- 5.0mm crochet hook
- Worsted weight yarn in green
- Embroidery floss in black
- 6mm black safety doll eyes, beads, or buttons
- Polyester stuffing material
- Embroidery needle

GAUGE

Varies

FINISHED SIZE

Approx. 3–5"

Body

R1–ch2, 6sc in 2nd chain from hook, mm

R2–2sc in each sc around (12sc), mm

R3–*2sc in 1st sc, 1sc in next sc, repeat from * around, mm

R4–in back loops only, sc in each stitch around, mm

R5 thru 11–sc in each stitch around, mm

R12–*sc2tog, 1sc, repeat from * around, FO

Stuff.

Head

R1–ch2, 6sc in 2nd chain from hook, mm

R2–2sc in each sc around (12sc), mm

R3–*2sc in 1st sc, 1sc in next, repeat from * around, mm

R4–*2sc in 1st sc, 1sc in next 2sc, repeat from * around, mm

R5–*2sc in 1st sc, 1sc in next 3sc, repeat from * around, mm

R6 thru 10–sc in each sc around, mm

R11–*sc2tog, 1sc in next 3sc, repeat from * around, mm

R12–*sc2tog, 1sc in next 2sc, repeat from * around, mm

R13–*sc2tog, 1sc in next sc, repeat from * around, mm

Stuff.

R14–sc2tog around, FO

If you're using snap-on doll eyes, remember to have them in place before stuffing or assembly.

Eyes (make 2)

Working in rounds

R1–ch2, 5sc in 1st chain from hook, mm

R2&3–sc in each sc around (5sc), FO

If you're using 6mm doll eyes, attach them now.

Arms (make 2)

ch3, sc in 2nd chain from hook, sc (2sc across), ch1, turn

*2 sc, ch1, turn

Repeat from * for 2 more rows (4 rows total)

2sc in each sc (4sc), ch1, turn

*sc, ch3, slip stitch in same space to form picot, repeat across from * (4 picot fingers), FO

Feet (make 2)

ch4, sc in 2nd chain from hook, sc across, ch1, turn

3sc across, ch1, turn, *sc, ch3, slip stitch in same space to form picot, repeat across from * (3 picot toes), FO

Sew appendages to head and body as shown in picture.

Weave in ends.

Using embroidery floss, make mouth as you wish.

$\mathcal{B}$eaver

MATERIALS

5.0mm crochet hook

Worsted weight yarn in light brown and off-white

Embroidery floss in black

6mm black safety doll eyes, beads, or buttons

Polyester stuffing material

Embroidery needle

GAUGE

Varies

FINISHED SIZE

Approx. 3–5"

Body

R1–ch2, 6sc in 2nd chain from hook, mm

R2–2sc in each sc around (12sc), mm

R3–*2sc in 1st sc, 1sc in next sc, repeat from * around, mm

R4–in back loops only, sc in each stitch around, mm

R5 thru 11–sc in each stitch around, mm

R12–*sc2tog, 1sc, repeat from * around, FO

Stuff.

Head

R1–ch2, 6sc in 2nd chain from hook, mm

R2–2sc in each sc around (12sc), mm

R3–*2sc in 1st sc, 1sc in next, repeat from * around, mm

R4–*2sc in 1st sc, 1sc in next 2sc, repeat from * around, mm

R5–*2sc in 1st sc, 1sc in next 3sc, repeat from * around, mm

R6 thru 10–sc in each sc around, mm

R11–*sc2tog, 1sc in next 3sc, repeat from * around, mm

R12–*sc2tog, 1sc in next 2sc, repeat from * around, mm

R13–*sc2tog, 1sc in next sc, repeat from * around, mm

Stuff.

R14–sc2tog around, FO

If you're using snap-on doll eyes, remember to have them in place before stuffing or assembly.

Cheeks (make 2)

Working in rounds

With light brown

R1–ch2, 5sc in 1st chain, mm

R2&3–sc in each sc around (5sc), FO

Teeth (make 2)

With off-white

ch2, 3sc in 2nd chain from hook, FO

Stitch up under cheeks . . . cute!

Ears (make 2)

With light brown

ch2, 3sc in 1st chain, ch1, turn

2sc in each sc, FO

Use tail to pinch the bottom edge, sew to head.

Arms (make 4)

Working in rounds

With light brown

R1–ch2, 5sc in 1st chain from hook, mm

R2–2sc in each sc around, mm

R3–working in back loops, sc around, mm

R4 thru 6–sc around, FO

Tail (make 2)

ch11, sc in 2nd chain from hook, sc across, ch2, working in back loops of base chain sc across, turn, sc9, 2sc in next 3 stitches, sc across, turn, 5sc, 2hdc, 2dc, 2tr, 2tr in next 3 stitches, 2tr, 2dc, 2hdc, 5sc, FO

Using slip stitch, stitch tails together leaving one open end at the base, FO.

Stuff tail lightly and sew to base of body.

Face

With embroidery floss, make nose. (You can also use doll eyes or buttons.)

With embroidery floss, make eyes. (You can also use doll eyes or buttons.)

Finishing

Sew appendages to head and body.

Weave in ends.

Koala

MATERIALS

5.0mm crochet hook

Worsted weight yarn in gray, white, and black

Embroidery floss

6mm black safety doll eyes, beads, or buttons

Polyester stuffing material

Embroidery needle

GAUGE

Varies

FINISHED SIZE

Approx. 3–5"

Body

With gray

R1–ch2, 6sc in 2nd chain from hook, mm

R2–2sc in each sc around (12sc), mm

R3–*2sc in 1st sc, 1sc in next sc, repeat from * around, mm

R4–in back loops only, sc in each stitch around, mm

R5 thru 11–sc in each stitch around, mm

R12–*sc2tog, 1sc, repeat from * around, FO

Stuff.

Head

With gray

R1–ch2, 6sc in 2nd chain from hook, mm

R2–2sc in each sc around (12sc), mm

R3–*2sc in 1st sc, 1sc in next, repeat from * around, mm

R4–*2sc in 1st sc, 1sc in next 2sc, repeat from * around, mm

R5–*2sc in 1st sc, 1sc in next 3sc, repeat from * around, mm

R6 thru 10–sc in each sc around, mm

R11–*sc2tog, 1sc in next 3sc, repeat from * around, mm

R12–*sc2tog, 1sc in next 2sc, repeat from * around, mm

R13–*sc2tog, 1sc in next sc, repeat from * around, mm

Stuff.

R14–sc2tog around, FO

> *If you're using snap-on doll eyes, remember to have them in place before stuffing or assembly.*

Ears (make 2)

With white

ch2, 3sc in 2nd chain from hook, ch1, turn

2sc in each sc (6sc), FO

With gray

Join with sc in corner, 2sc in each sc (12sc), FO

Legs (make 4)

With gray

R1–ch2, 4sc in 2nd chain from hook, mm

R2–2sc in each sc around, mm

R3–working in the back loops in this round only, sc in each stitch around, mm

R4 thru 6–sc around, FO

Nose and Face

With black

ch3, sc 2 times, ch1, turn

2sc, ch1, turn, sc2tog, FO

Sew appendages to head and body as shown in picture.

Weave in ends.

Sew onto face as shown.

Use embroidery floss, beads, buttons, or doll eyes to make eyes.

Hippo

MATERIALS

5.0mm crochet hook

Worsted weight yarn in light blue

Embroidery floss

6mm black safety doll eyes, beads, or buttons

Polyester stuffing material

Embroidery needle

GAUGE

Varies

FINISHED SIZE

Approx. 3–5"

Body

R1–ch2, 6sc in 2nd chain from hook, mm

R2–2sc in each sc around (12sc), mm

R3–*2sc in 1st sc, 1sc in next sc, repeat from * around, mm

R4–in back loops only, sc in each stitch around, mm

R5 thru 11–sc in each stitch around, mm

R12–*sc2tog, 1sc, repeat from * around, FO

Stuff.

Head

R1–ch2, 6sc in 2nd chain from hook, mm

R2–2sc in each sc around (12sc), mm

R3–*2sc in 1st sc, 1sc in next, repeat from * around, mm

R4–*2sc in 1st sc, 1sc in next 2sc, repeat from * around, mm

R5–*2sc in 1st sc, 1sc in next 3sc, repeat from * around, mm

R6 thru 10–sc in each sc around, mm

R11–*sc2tog, 1sc in next 3sc, repeat from * around, mm

R12–*sc2tog, 1sc in next 2sc, repeat from * around, mm

R13–*sc2tog, 1sc in next sc, repeat from * around, mm

Stuff.

R14–sc2tog around, FO

If you're using snap-on doll eyes, remember to have them in place before stuffing or assembly.

Ears (make 2)

ch2, 3sc in 2nd chain from hook, ch1, turn

2sc in each sc, FO

Use tail to pinch the bottom edge, sew to head.

Arms (make 4)

Working in rounds

R1–ch2, 5sc in 2nd chain from hook, mm

R2–2sc in each sc around, mm

R3–working in back loops, sc around, mm

R4 thru 6–sc around, FO

Muzzle

Working in rounds

R1–ch7, sc in 2nd chain from hook, 6 sc, ch2, 6sc, ch2, mm

R2–*sc5, 2sc in next 3 stitches, repeat from * mm

R3 thru 5–sc around, mm

R6–*sc2tog, 2sc, repeat from * around, mm

R7–*sc2tog, 1sc, repeat from * around, FO

Face

With embroidery floss, make nostrils and smile.

With embroidery floss, make eyes. (You can also use doll eyes or buttons.)

Finishing

Sew appendages to head and body as shown in picture.

Weave in ends.

Lemur

MATERIALS

5.0mm crochet hook

Worsted weight yarn in gray, white, and black

Embroidery floss

12mm brown and black doll eyes

Snap-on doll nose

Polyester stuffing material

Embroidery needle

GAUGE

Varies

FINISHED SIZE

Approx. 3–5"

Body

With gray

R1–ch2, 6sc in 2nd chain from hook, mm

R2–2sc in each sc around (12sc), mm

R3–*2sc in 1st sc, 1sc in next sc, repeat from * around, mm

R4–in back loops only, sc in each stitch around, mm

R5 thru 11–sc in each stitch around, mm

R12–*sc2tog, 1sc, repeat from * around, FO

Stuff.

Head

With gray

R1–ch2, 6sc in 2nd chain from hook, mm

R2–2sc in each sc around (12sc), mm

R3–*2sc in 1st sc, 1sc in next, repeat from * around, mm

R4–*2sc in 1st sc, 1sc in next 2sc, repeat from * around, mm

R5–*2sc in 1st sc, 1sc in next 3sc, repeat from * around, mm

R6 thru 10–sc in each sc around, mm

R11–*sc2tog, 1sc in next 3sc, repeat from * around, mm

R12–*sc2tog, 1sc in next 2sc, repeat from * around, mm

R13–*sc2tog, 1sc in next sc, repeat from * around, mm

Stuff.

R14–sc2tog around, FO

> *If you're using snap-on doll eyes, remember to have them in place before stuffing or assembly.*

Ears (make 2)

With white

ch2, 3sc in 2nd chain from hook, ch1, turn

2sc in each sc, FO

With black

Join at corner with a sc.

2sc in each sc, FO

Use tail to pinch the bottom edge, sew to head.

Eyes (make 2)

With black

ch3, 12dc in 2nd chain from hook, join to 1st stitch with
slip stitch to form ring, FO

Slip doll eye through hole, snap in place.

Tail

Section 1

With white

R1–ch2, 5sc in 2nd chain from hook, mm

R2–2 sc in each sc around, mm

R3–sc around, FO

Section 2

With black

R1–join with sc in any sc, sc around, mm

R2–sc around, mm

R3–sc around, FO

Section 3

With white

> R1–join with sc in any sc, sc around, mm
>
> R2–sc around, mm
>
> R3–sc around, FO

Sections 4 thru 8

> Repeat section 3, alternating between
> black and white, FO

Section 9

With gray

> R1–join with sc in any sc, sc around, mm
>
> R2–sc around, mm
>
> R3–slip stitch in next 5sc, sc in last 5sc, mm

Now working in rows

> R1–sc in the 5sc, ch1, turn
>
> R2 thru 4–sc across, ch1, turn
>
> R5–sc across, FO
>
> To attach tail, refer to picture.

Arms (make 4)

Working in rounds

With black

> R1–ch2, 5sc in 2nd chain from hook, mm
>
> R2–2sc in each sc around, mm
>
> R3–working in back loops, sc around, mm
>
> R4–sc around, FO

With gray

> Join with sc in any sc, sc around, FO
>
> Stuff and sew to body.

Face

With felt, cut out 2 circles and sew to face as shown.

> With embroidery floss, make nose.
>
> With embroidery floss, make eyes.
>
> > *Or you can use doll eyes or buttons instead. The photo shows doll eyes and a doll nose to make the face, but stitching with embroidery floss works well, too.*

Finishing

> Sew appendages to head and body.
>
> Weave in ends.

Bumblebee

MATERIALS

   4.0mm crochet hook

   Worsted weight yarn in black, yellow, and white

   Embroidery floss in black

   6mm black safety doll eyes, beads, or buttons

   Polyester stuffing material

   Embroidery needle

GAUGE

   4.5 stitches x 5 rows = 1"

FINISHED SIZE

   Approx. 4" from head to tail

Body

With black

   R1–ch2, sc 7 times in 2nd chain from hook, mm (with slip stitch here and throughout)

   R2–sc around, mm

   R3–sc around, mm

   R4–2sc in each sc around, mm

   R5–*2sc in 1st stitch, 1sc in next stitch, repeat from * around, mm

   R6–*2sc in 1st stitch, 1sc in next 2 stitches, repeat from * around, mm

   R7–*2sc in 1st stitch, 1sc in next 3 stitches, repeat from * around, mm

   R8 thru 11–sc around, FO

With yellow

   R12–join with sc in any stitch, sc around, mm

   R13 thru 17–sc around, FO

With black

   R18–join with sc in any stitch, sc around, mm

   R19–sc around, mm

   R20–*sc2tog, sc in next 3 stitches, repeat from * around, mm

   R21–*sc2tog, sc in next 2 stitches, repeat from * around, mm

   R22–*sc2tog, sc in next stitch, repeat from * around, mm
   Stuff.

   R23–sc2tog around, FO

Head

With yellow

   R1–ch2, sc 5 times in 2nd chain from hook, mm (with slip stitch here and throughout)

   R2–*2sc in 1st stitch, 1sc in next stitch, repeat from * around, mm

   R3&4–sc around, mm

   R5–*sc2tog, sc in next stitch, repeat from * around, mm

   If you are using doll eyes, snap into place now.
   Stuff.

   R6–sc2tog around, FO

   Sew head to body with tail.

Wings (make 2)

With white

   R1–ch2, sc 6 times in 2nd chain from hook, mm (with slip stitch here and throughout)

   R2–2sc in each sc around, mm

   R3–*2sc in 1st stitch, 1sc in next stitch, repeat from * to last 3 stitches, slip stitch in last 3 stitches, FO

   Sew to body.

Antennae (make 2)

With black embroidery floss and your crochet hook.

   Add a 3" length of floss like a tassel to the top of the head. Tie a knot in the end about 1" from the top of the head. Trim excess.

   If you make the antennae too long, they might droop.

   If you make them too short, they might look like horns.

   Don't be afraid to try multiple times, until you get them just to your liking.

$\mathcal{P}$up

MATERIALS

4.0mm crochet hook

Worsted weight yarn in lavender and sage green

Embroidery floss in black and white

Polyester stuffing material

Polyester beads for stuffing

Embroidery needle

GAUGE

24 stitches x 24 rows = 4"

FINISHED SIZE

Approx. 4.5"

Head

With lavender

R1–ch2, 6sc in 2nd chain from hook, mm

R2–2sc in each sc around (12sc), mm

R3–*2sc in 1st sc, 1sc in next, repeat from * around, mm

R4–*2sc in 1st sc, 1sc in next 2sc, repeat from * around, mm

R5–*2sc in 1st sc, 1sc in next 3sc, repeat from * around, mm

R6–*2sc in 1st sc, 1sc in next 4sc, repeat from * around, mm

R7 thru R13–sc in each stitch around, mm

R14–*sc2tog, 1sc in next 4sc, repeat from * around, mm

R15–*sc2tog, 1sc in next 3sc, repeat from * around, mm

R16–*sc2tog, 1sc in next 2sc, repeat from * around, mm

R17–*sc2tog, 1sc in next sc, repeat from * around, FO

Stuff firmly.

Set aside.

Body

With lavender

R1–ch2, 6sc in 2nd chain from hook, mm

R2–2sc in each sc around (12sc), mm

R3–*2sc in 1st sc, 1sc in next, repeat from * around, mm

R4 thru 13–sc in each stitch around, FO

Stuff body with poly beads.

Attach head to body using whip stitch.

Arms and Legs (make 4)

With sage green

R1–ch2, 6sc in 2nd chain from hook, mm

R2 thru 6–sc in each stitch around, FO

No need to stuff the arms and legs.

Use tail to stitch up the tiny hole where you finished off. You should be left with a little appendage that looks like a sausage.

For the legs, stitch to the sides of the body section near the bottom (not to the bottom of the body).

For the arms, stitch into the crux of the neck.

Refer to the chart on page 5 for placement of appendages.

Ears (make 2)

With sage green

R1–ch2, 6sc in 2nd chain from hook, mm

R2 thru 10–sc in each stitch around, FO

Stitch onto the top of the head. Refer to pictures for placement.

Nose

With 2 strands of sage green yarn, stitch an upside-down triangle in the center of the face.

In the photo, the nose is 2 rows high and 4 stitches wide at the widest point.

Eyes

With 2 strands of black embroidery floss, stitch on 2 circles parallel to the top of the nose. Add 3 eyelashes and, with 3 strands of white embroidery floss, stitch a twinkle in each eye.

$\mathcal{O}$wl

MATERIALS

5.0mm crochet hook

Worsted weight yarn in gold, pink, and green

12mm doll eyes

Polyester stuffing material

Embroidery needle

GAUGE

3 stitches x 4 rows = 1"

FINISHED SIZE

Approx. wingspan 8"; height 4.5"

Top of the Body

With gold

R1–ch2, 6hdc in 1st chain from hook, mm

Work in the back loops from this point on

R2–ch1, 2hdc in each hdc around (12hdc), mm

R3–*2hdc in 1st hdc, 1hdc in next, repeat from * around, mm

R4–*2hdc in 1st hdc, 1hdc in next 2hdc, repeat from * around, mm

R5–*2hdc in 1st hdc, 1hdc in next 3hdc, repeat from * around, mm

R6–hdc in each stitch around, mm

R7–*2hdc in 1st hdc, 1hdc in next 4hdc, repeat from * around, mm

R8–hdc in each stitch around, mm

R9–*2hdc in 1st hdc, 1hdc in next 5hdc, repeat from * around, mm

R10–hdc in each stitch around, mm

R11–*2hdc in 1st hdc, 1hdc in next 6hdc, repeat from * around, mm

R12 thru 14–hdc in each stitch around, mm, FO

Eyes (make 2)

With pink

ch2, 12dc in 1st chain from hook, join with slip stitch to form ring, FO

Slip stitch in 12mm doll eyes and lock into place on the body.

Bottom of the Body

With pink

R1–ch2, 6sc in 1st chain from hook, mm

R2–2sc in each sc around (12sc), mm

R3–*2sc in 1st sc, 1sc in next, repeat from * around, mm

R4–*2sc in 1st sc, 1sc in next 2sc, repeat from * around, mm

R5–*2sc in 1st sc, 1sc in next 3sc, repeat from * around, mm

R6–*2sc in 1st sc, 1sc in next 4sc, repeat from * around, mm

R7–*2sc in 1st sc, 1sc in next 5sc, repeat from * around, mm

R8–*2sc in 1st sc, 1sc in next 6sc, repeat from * around, mm

Make sure eyes are in place before closing.

Attach bottom to top with a whip stitch, leaving a small hole. Stuff, then close.

Nose

With green

ch6, sc in 2nd chain from hook and across (5sc), ch1, turn
sc2tog, sc across, ch1, turn (4sc)
Repeat until you are down to 1sc, FO
Stitch to face between eyes.

Wings

With pink

The wings are made with feathers that are overlapped,
then stitched together and stitched to the body.

Feather 1

ch9, sc in 2nd chain from hook and in next 7 stitches, 4sc
in same stitch, 8sc in the bottom loops of the chain

Feather 2

ch7, sc in 2nd chain from hook and in next 5 stitches, 4sc
in same stitch, 6sc in the bottom loops of the chain

Feather 3

ch5, sc in 2nd chain from hook and in next 3 stitches, 4sc
in same stitch, 4sc in the bottom loops of the chain

Example of Feather Making

Dash = ch
X = sc

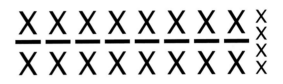

$\mathcal{B}$ear

MATERIALS

4.0mm crochet hook

Worsted weight yarn in dark pink and turquoise

Embroidery floss in black

Polyester stuffing material

Polyester beads for stuffing

Embroidery needle

GAUGE

24 stitches x 24 rows = 4"

FINISHED SIZE

Approx. 4.5"

Head

With dark pink

R1–ch2, 6sc in 2nd chain from hook, mm

R2–2sc in each sc around (12sc), mm

R3–*2sc in 1st sc, 1sc in next, repeat from * around, mm

R4–*2sc in 1st sc, 1sc in next 2sc, repeat from * around, mm

R5–*2sc in 1st sc, 1sc in next 3sc, repeat from * around, mm

R6–*2sc in 1st sc, 1sc in next 4sc, repeat from * around, mm

R7 thru R13–sc in each stitch around, mm

R14–*sc2tog, 1sc in next 4sc, repeat from * around, mm

R15–*sc2tog, 1sc in next 3sc, repeat from * around, mm

R16–*sc2tog, 1sc in next 2sc, repeat from * around, mm

R17–*sc2tog, 1sc in next sc, repeat from * around, FO

Stuff firmly.

Set aside.

Body

With dark pink

R1–ch2, 6sc in 2nd chain from hook, mm

R2–2sc in each sc around (12sc), mm

R3–*2sc in 1st sc, 1sc in next, repeat from * around, mm

R4 thru 13–sc in each stitch around, FO

Stuff body with poly beads.

Attach head to body using whip stitch.

Arms and Legs (make 4)

With turquoise

R1–ch2, 6sc in 2nd chain from hook, mm

R2 thru 6–sc in each stitch around, FO

No need to stuff the arms and legs.

Use tail to stitch up the hole where you finished off. You should be left with a little appendage that looks like a sausage.

For the legs, stitch to the sides of the body near the bottom (not to the bottom of the body).

For the arms, stitch into the crux of the neck.

Refer to the chart on page 5 for placement of appendages.

Ears (make 2)

With turquoise

R1–ch2, 6sc in 2nd chain from hook, mm

R2&3–sc in each stitch around, FO

Stitch onto the top of the head.

Nose

With 2 strands of turquoise yarn, stitch an upside-down triangle in the center of the face.

In the photo, the nose is 2 rows high and 4 stitches wide at the widest point.

Eyes

With 3 strands of black embroidery floss, backstitch on 2 slits 3 stitches wide. You may want to make the line thicker to accentuate.

Mouth

With 3 strands of black embroidery floss, stitch a small mouth.

Penguin

MATERIALS

4.0mm crochet hook

Worsted weight yarn in light gray, off-white, and black

6mm black safety doll eyes, beads, or buttons

Polyester stuffing material

Polyester beads for stuffing

Embroidery needle

GAUGE

20 rows x 20 stitches = 4"

FINISHED SIZE

Approx. 3.5" tall

Head

With off-white

R1–ch2, 6sc in 2nd chain from hook, mm

R2–2sc in each sc around (12sc), mm

R3–*2sc in 1st sc, 1sc in next, repeat from * around, mm

R4–*2sc in 1st sc, 1sc in next 2sc, repeat from * around, mm

R5–*2sc in 1st sc, 1sc in next 3sc, repeat from * around, mm

R6 thru 10–sc in each stitch around, mm

R11–*sc2tog, 1sc in next 3sc, repeat from * around, mm

R12–*sc2tog, 1sc in next 2sc, repeat from * around, mm

Insert eyes low on the head and wide-set.

R13–*sc2tog, 1sc in next sc, repeat from * around, FO

Body

With light gray

R1–ch2, 6sc in 2nd chain from hook, mm

R2–2sc in each sc around (12sc), mm

R3–*2sc in 1st sc, 1sc in next, repeat from * around, mm

R4–*2sc in 1st sc, 1sc in next 2sc, repeat from * around, mm

R5–*2sc in 1st sc, 1sc in next 3sc, repeat from * around, mm

R6–*2sc in 1st sc, 1sc in next 4sc, repeat from * around, mm

R7–*2sc in 1st sc, 1sc in next 5sc, repeat from * around, mm

R8–in the back loops in this round only, sc in each stitch around, mm

R9 thru 12–sc in each stitch around, mm

R13–*sc2tog, 1sc in next 5sc, repeat from * around, mm

R14&15–sc in each stitch around, mm

R16–*sc2tog, 1sc in next 4sc, repeat from * around, mm

R17&18–sc in each stitch around, mm

R19–*sc2tog, 1sc in next 3sc, repeat from * around, mm

R20–sc in each stitch around, mm

R21–*sc2tog, 1sc in next 2sc, repeat from * around, FO

Fill bottom with polyester beads and top off with polyester stuffing.

Stuff head and sew to body.

Black Hood

With black

ch24, slip stitch in 1st chain from hook to form ring

work 2 rounds of sc (24sc)

Working in rows

R1–sc 10, ch1, turn

R2–sc across, ch1, turn

R3–sc2tog, 6sc, sc2tog, ch1, turn (8sc)

R4–sc across, ch1, turn

R5–sc2tog, 4sc, sc2tog, ch1, turn (6sc)

R6 thru 15–sc across, ch1, turn

R16–sc2tog, 2sc, sc2tog, ch1, turn (4sc)

R17&18–sc across, FO with a very long tail

Slip hood over the head and stitch in place along the edges.

Beak

With black

ch3, sc in 2nd chain from hook, sc across (2sc), ch1, turn,
  sc2tog, ch1, turn, sc, FO

Stitch beak in place.

Wings (make 2)

With light gray

R1–ch2, 6sc in 2nd chain from hook, mm

R2&3–sc in each stitch around, mm

R4–*2sc in 1st sc, 1sc in next, repeat from * around, mm

R5&6–sc in each stitch around, mm

R7–*2sc in 1st sc, 2sc in next, repeat from * around, mm

R8&9–sc in each stitch around, mm

R10–*2sc in 1st sc, 3sc in next, repeat from * around, mm

R11&12–sc in each stitch around, FO

Stitch to the base of the neck and tack down the tips of
  the wings to the sides with 1 or 2 stitches.

Turtle

MATERIALS

5.0mm crochet hook

Worsted weight yarn in light blue, red, pink, and white

9mm black doll eyes

Polyester stuffing material

Embroidery needle

GAUGE

20 rows x 20 stitches = 4"

FINISHED SIZE

Approx. 3.5" tall x 5" long

Shell

With red

R1–ch2, 6hdc in 1st chain from hook, mm

Working in the back loops from this point on

R2–ch1, 2hdc in each hdc around (12hdc), mm

R3–*2hdc in 1st hdc, 1hdc in next, repeat from * around, mm

R4–*2hdc in 1st hdc, 1hdc in next 2hdc, repeat from * around, mm

R5–*2hdc in 1st hdc, 1hdc in next 3hdc, repeat from * around, mm

R6–*2hdc in 1st hdc, 1hdc in next 4hdc, repeat from * around, mm

R7 thru 10–hdc in each hdc around, FO

Belly

With pink

R1–ch2, 6sc in 2nd chain from hook, mm

R2–2sc in each sc around (12sc), mm

R3–*2sc in 1st sc, 1sc in next, repeat from * around, mm

R4–*2sc in 1st sc, 1sc in next 2sc, repeat from * around, mm

R5–*2sc in 1st sc, 1sc in next 3sc, repeat from * around, mm

R6–*2sc in 1st sc, 1sc in next 4sc, repeat from * around, FO

Attach belly and shell using whip stitch.

Stuff.

Eyes (make 2)

With off-white

R1–ch2, work 6sc in ring then 6dc in ring, join with slip stitch to form ring, FO

Slip doll eyes into the holes without snapping them shut.

Set aside.

Head

With light blue

R1–ch2, 6sc in 2nd chain from hook, mm

R2–2sc in each sc around (12sc), mm

R3–*2sc in 1st sc, 1sc in next, repeat from * around, mm

R4–*2sc in 1st sc, 1sc in next 2sc, repeat from * around, mm

R5–*2sc in 1st sc, 1sc in next 3sc, repeat from * around, mm

R6 thru 10–sc in each stitch around, mm

R11–*sc2tog, 1sc in next 3sc, repeat from * around, mm

R12–*sc2tog, 1sc in next 2sc, repeat from * around, mm

Attach eyes.

R13–*sc2tog, 1sc in next sc, repeat from * around, FO

Neck

With light blue

ch8, slip stitch in 1st chain to form ring, ch1, sc in each stitch around (8sc), ch1, work 2 more rounds, ch1, sc in next 4 stitches, ch1, turn, work 1 more row, FO

Legs (make 4)

With light blue

R1–ch2, 8sc in 2nd chain from hook, mm

R2–in back loops, sc in each stitch around, mm

R3–sc around, mm

R4–sc in next 4 stitches, ch1, turn

R5–sc across (4sc), FO

Tail

With light blue

ch5, join slip stitch in 1st chain to form ring, ch1, turn, sc
around, ch1, sc around, ch1, turn, sc2tog around, FO

Embellishment

To make the off-white circles

Small

ch2, 6sc in 2nd chain from hook, join slip stitch in 1st stitch
to form ring, FO

Medium

ch2, 8hdc in 2nd chain from hook, join slip stitch in 1st
stitch to form ring, FO

Large

R1–ch2, 6sc in 2nd chain from hook, mm

R2–2sc in each sc around (12sc), FO

Stitch on side of shell as in pattern shown . . .
or create your own!

Fox

MATERIALS

4.0mm crochet hook

Worsted weight yarn in orange-red, off-white, and black

6mm black safety doll eyes, beads, or buttons

Polyester stuffing material

Polyester beads for stuffing

Embroidery needle

GAUGE

22 rows x 22 stitches = 4"

FINISHED SIZE

Approx. 7" long x 3" tall

Eyes (make 2)

With off-white

ch2, 8hdc in 2nd chain from hook, join with slip stitch in
1st hdc, FO

Slip eyes in center of ring.

Set aside.

Snout

With off-white

R1–ch2, 6sc in 2nd chain from hook, mm

R2&3–sc in each stitch around, mm

R4–*2sc in 1st sc, 1sc in next, repeat from * around, mm

R5&6–sc in each stitch around, mm

R7–*2sc in 1st sc, 1sc in next 2sc, repeat from * around, mm

R8–sc in each stitch around, mm

R9–*2sc in 1st sc, 1sc in next 3sc, repeat from * around, mm

R10–sc in each stitch around, FO

Stuff.

Set aside.

Head

With orange-red

R1–ch2, 6sc in 2nd chain from hook, mm

R2–2sc in each sc around (12sc), mm

R3–*2sc in 1st sc, 1sc in next, repeat from * around, mm

R4–*2sc in 1st sc, 1sc in next 2sc, repeat from * around, mm

R5–*2sc in 1st sc, 1sc in next 3sc, repeat from * around, mm

R6–*2sc in 1st sc, 1sc in next 4sc, repeat from * around, mm

R7 thru 12–sc in each stitch around, mm

R14–*sc2tog, 1sc in next 4sc, repeat from * around, mm

R15–*sc2tog, 1sc in next 3sc, repeat from * around, mm

R16–*sc2tog, 1sc in next 2sc, repeat from * around, mm

Attach eyes.

R17–*sc2tog, 1sc in next sc, repeat from * around, FO

Stuff firmly.

Attach snout with 2 strands of black yarn, stitch on nose.

Ears (make 2)

With orange-red

R1–ch2, 6sc in 2nd chain from hook, mm

R2&3–sc in each stitch around, mm

R4–*2sc in 1st sc, 1sc in next, repeat from * around, mm

R5–sc in each stitch around, mm

R6–*2sc in 1st sc, 1sc in next, repeat from * around, mm

R7–sc in each stitch around, mm

R8–*2sc in 1st sc, 1sc in next, repeat from * around, mm

R9 thru 11–sc in each stitch around, mm

R12–*sc2tog, 1sc in next sc, repeat from * around, FO

Body

With orange-red

R1–ch2, 6sc in 2nd chain from hook, mm

R2–2sc in each sc around (12sc), mm

R3–*2sc in 1st sc, 1sc in next, repeat from * around, mm

R4 thru 12–sc in each stitch around, mm

R13–2sc in 1st 6 stitches, sc around remaining stitches, mm

R14 thru 19–sc in each stitch around, mm

R20–sc2tog around, mm

R21–sc2tog around, FO

Stuff.

Front Legs (make 2)

With orange-red

R1–ch2, 3sc and 3dc in 2nd chain from hook, mm

R2–3sc and 3hdc, mm

R3 thru 7–sc in each stitch around, FO leaving a long tail

Close hole with tail and sew to the sides of the front of body.

Back Legs (make 2)

With orange-red

R1–ch2, 3sc and 3dc in 2nd chain from hook, mm

R2–3sc and 3hdc, mm

R3 thru 7–sc in each stitch around, mm

R8–*2sc in 1st sc, 1sc in next, repeat from * around, mm

R9–sc2tog around, FO

Close hole with tail and sew to the sides of the back of body.

Tail

With off-white

R1–ch2, 6sc in 2nd chain from hook, mm

R2–sc in each stitch around, mm

R3–*2sc in 1st sc, 1sc in next, repeat from * around, mm

R4–sc in each stitch around, mm

R5–*2sc in 1st sc, 2sc in next, repeat from * around, mm

R6–*sc, dc, sc, repeat from * around, mm

R7–join orange-red, *sc, dc, sc, repeat from * around, mm

R8–*2sc in 1st sc, 3sc in next, repeat from * around, mm

R9 thru 17–sc in each stitch around, mm

R18–*sc2tog, 1sc in next 3sc, repeat from * around, mm

R19–*sc2tog, 1sc in next 2sc, repeat from * around, mm

R20–*sc2tog, 1sc in next sc, repeat from * around, FO

Stitch to end of body.

Hedgehog

MATERIALS

4.0mm crochet hook

Worsted weight yarn in off-white, light brown, and black

Eyelash yarn in dark brown

6mm black safety doll eyes, beads, or buttons

Polyester stuffing material

Polyester beads for stuffing

Embroidery needle

GAUGE

20 stitches x 22 rows = 4"

FINISHED SIZE

Approx. 2" tall x 5" long

Body

With dark brown

R1–ch2, 6sc in 2nd chain from hook, mm

R2–*2sc in 1st sc, 1sc in next, repeat from * around, mm

R3&4–sc in each stitch around, mm

R5–*2sc in 1st sc, 1sc in next 2sc, repeat from * around, mm

R6&7–sc in each stitch around, mm

R8–*2sc in 1st sc, 1sc in next 3sc, repeat from * around, mm

R9 thru 18–sc in each stitch around, mm

R19–sc2tog around, mm

Stuff halfway with poly beads first, then top off with
   stuffing.

R20–sc2tog around, FO

Close hole.

Face

With off-white

R1–ch2, 6sc in 2nd chain from hook, mm

R2 thru 5–sc in each stitch around, mm

R6–*2sc in 1st sc, 1sc in next, repeat from * around, mm

R7&8–sc in each stitch around, mm

R9–*2sc in 1st sc, 1sc in next, repeat from * around, mm

R10&11–sc in each stitch around, mm

R12–*2sc in 1st sc, 1sc in next, repeat from * around, mm

R13&14–sc in each stitch around

R15–*2sc in 1st sc, 1sc in next 2sc, repeat from * around, FO

Attach eyes on either side of the face.

Stuff and stitch face onto body hiding the decreased end
   behind the face.

With 2 strands of black yarn stitch on nose.

How to Add Fur

To add fur, pick up stitches (see the lion pattern on page
   34 for reference) and work in sc rows, back and forth
   on the back side of the body, leaving the belly side
   exposed, from the tail end up. Stop when you get to
   the base of the face portion. Fluff fur with your fingers
   to hide stitches.

Feet (make 4)

With light brown

R1–ch2, 6sc in 2nd chain from hook, mm

R2 thru 4–sc in each stitch around, FO

Stitch to underside of the belly.

   *Be aware of spacing so your doll doesn't tip forward at the
   nose.*

Octopus

MATERIALS

- 4.0mm crochet hook
- Worsted weight yarn in off-white
- Embroidery floss in red
- 12mm black doll eyes
- Polyester stuffing material
- Embroidery needle

GAUGE

24 rows x 22 stitches = 4"

FINISHED SIZE

Approx. 3" tall

Body

R1–ch2, 8sc in 2nd chain from hook, mm

R2–2sc in each sc around (16sc), mm

R3–*2sc in 1st sc, 1sc in next, repeat from * around, mm

R4–*2sc in 1st sc, 1sc in next 2sc, repeat from * around, mm

R5–*2sc in 1st sc, 1sc in next 3sc, repeat from * around, mm

R6–*2sc in 1st sc, 1sc in next 4sc, repeat from * around, mm

R7 thru 16–sc in each stitch around, mm

R14–*sc2tog, 1sc in next 4sc, repeat from * around, mm

R15–*sc2tog, 1sc in next 3sc, repeat from * around, mm

R16–*sc2tog, 1sc in next 2sc, repeat from * around, mm

Insert eyes.

R17–*sc2tog, 1sc in next sc, repeat from * around, FO

Stuff firmly.

Legs (make 8)

R1–ch2, 8sc in 2nd chain from hook, mm

R2–2sc in each sc around (16sc), mm

R3&4–sc in each stitch around, mm

R5–sc2tog around, FO

Stitch to bottom of body evenly spaced and in a circular pattern.

Face

With red embroidery floss, stitch a *V*-shaped mouth between the eyes.

Fish

MATERIALS

4.0mm crochet hook

Worsted weight yarn in gold and off-white

Embroidery floss in black and red

Polyester stuffing material

Embroidery needle

GAUGE

20 stitches x 22 rows = 4"

FINISHED SIZE

Approx. 5" long x 3" tall

Body

With gold

R1–ch2, 6sc in 2nd chain from hook, mm

R2&3–sc in each stitch around, mm

R4–*2sc in 1st sc, 1sc in next, repeat from * around, mm

R5&6–sc in each stitch around, mm

R7–*2sc in 1st sc, 1sc in next, repeat from * around, mm

R8&9–sc in each stitch around, mm

R10–*2sc in 1st sc, 1sc in next, repeat from * around, mm

R11&12–sc in each stitch around, mm

R13–*2sc in 1st sc, 2sc in next, repeat from * around, mm

R14 thru 17–sc in each stitch around, mm

R18–*2sc in 1st sc, 3sc in next, repeat from * around, mm

R19 thru 22–sc in each stitch around, FO

Face

With off-white

R1–ch2, 6sc in 2nd chain from hook, mm

R2–2sc in each sc around (12sc), mm

R3–*2sc in 1st sc, 1sc in next, repeat from * around, mm

R4–*2sc in 1st sc, 1sc in next 2sc, repeat from * around, mm

R5–*2sc in 1st sc, 1sc in next 3sc, repeat from * around, mm

R6–*2sc in 1st sc, 1sc in next 4sc, repeat from * around, mm

R7 thru 9–sc in each stitch around, FO

Stuff body and stitch face onto body.

Tail and Side Fins
(make 4: 2 gold and 2 off-white)

ch3, hdc in 3rd chain from hook, dc in same stitch, tr in same stitch, FO

Stitch gold fins to the tail and off-white fins onto the sides.

Top Fin

With gold

ch8, sc in 2nd chain from hook, hdc in next stitch, dc, tr, dc, hdc, sc, FO

Stitch to top of body section.

Eyes

With black embroidery floss, stitch 2 widely spaced circles 2 stitches wide and 3 stitches high. With 1 strand of the black floss, stitch on 3 eyelashes. With 2 strands of white, stitch a sparkle in each eye.

Mouth

With 2 strands of red floss, stitch a heart-shaped mouth, 3 stitches wide and 1.5 stitches high.

$\mathcal{M}$ouse

MATERIALS

- 4.0mm crochet hook
- Worsted weight yarn in dark gray, off-white, fuchsia, and black
- 6mm black safety doll eyes, beads, or buttons
- Polyester stuffing material
- Polyester beads for stuffing
- Embroidery needle

GAUGE

20 stitches x 22 rows = 4"

FINISHED SIZE

Approx. 2" tall x 4.5" long

Body

With dark gray

R1–ch2, 6sc in 2nd chain from hook, mm

R2–*2sc in 1st sc, 1sc in next, repeat from * around, mm

R3&4–sc in each stitch around, mm

R5–*2sc in 1st sc, 1sc in next 2sc, repeat from * around, mm

R6&7–sc in each stitch around, mm

R8–*2sc in 1st sc, 1sc in next 3sc, repeat from * around, mm

R9 thru 18–sc in each stitch around, mm

R19–sc2tog around, mm

Stuff halfway with poly beads first, then top off with stuffing.

R20–sc2tog around, FO

Close hole.

Face

With off-white

R1–ch2, 6sc in 2nd chain from hook, mm

R2 thru 4–sc in each stitch around, mm

R5–*2sc in 1st sc, 1sc in next, repeat from * around, mm

R6–sc in each stitch around, mm

R7–*2sc in 1st sc, 1sc in next, repeat from * around, mm

R8–sc in each stitch around, mm

R9–*2sc in 1st sc, 1sc in next, repeat from * around, mm

R10–sc in each stitch around, mm

R11–*2sc in 1st sc, 1sc in next 2sc, repeat from * around, mm

R12&13–sc in each stitch around, FO

Attach eyes on either side of the face.

Stuff and stitch face onto body hiding the decreased end behind the face.

With 2 strands of black yarn stitch on nose.

Feet (make 4)

With gray

R1–ch2, 6sc in 2nd chain from hook, mm

R2 thru 4–sc in each stitch around, FO

Stitch to underside of the belly.

Be aware of spacing so your doll doesn't tip forward at the nose.

Ears (make 2)

With fuchsia

R1–ch2, 6sc in 2nd chain from hook, mm

R2–2sc in each sc around (12sc), mm

R3–*2sc in 1st sc, 1sc in next, repeat from * around, mm

R4 thru 6–sc in each stitch around, mm

R7–*sc2tog, 1sc in next sc, repeat from * around, mm

R8–sc2tog around, FO

Flatten ball and stitch to body at the junction between the face and the body.

Tail

With fuchsia

Make a chain of 20 stitches, FO, and trim leaving ½" excess.

Fluff excess with fingers to create a little tuft.

Resources

For more patterns like the ones in this book, visit my website:

Roxycraft . . . Patterns That Don't Suck!

www.roxycraft.com

Yarn Websites

Misshawklet Yarn

www.misshawklet.com

Lion Brand Yarn Company

www.lionbrand.com

Crochet Resources on the Web

Crochet Guild of America

www.crochet.org

About.com

crochet.about.com

Amigurumi Resources on the Web

Crochet Me Magazine

www.crochetme.com/amigurumi

Our Models Are Wearing...

Bear: Lion brand Wool-Ease Worsted in Turquoise #620–148 and Azalea Pink #620–195.

Beaver: Lion brand Wool-Ease Worsted in Mushroom #620–403 and Fisherman #620–099.

Bumblebee: Lion brand Wool-Ease Worsted in Buttercup #620–158, Black #620–153, and Fisherman #620–099.

Elephant: Lion brand Wool-Ease Worsted in Azalea Pink #620–195.

Fish: Lion brand Wool-Ease Worsted in Gold #620–171 and Fisherman #620–099.

Fox: Lion brand Wool-Ease Worsted in Paprika #620–188, Fisherman #620–099, and Black #620–153.

Frog: Frog #1: Wool yarn by www.misshawklet.com. Frog #2: Lamb's Pride Worsted Weight Yarn in Limeade #M120.

Hedgehog: Lion brand Wool-Ease Worsted in Mushroom #620–403, Black #620–153, and Fisherman #620–099; Stylecraft Eskimo Eyelash yarn in Chocolate #5067.

Hippo: Lion brand Wool-Ease Worsted in Sea Spray #620–123.

Koala: Lion brand Wool-Ease Worsted in Gray Heather #620–151, Black #620–153, and Fisherman #620–099.

Lamb: Lamb #1: Lion brand Wool-Ease Worsted in Fisherman 620–099 and Oxford Gray 620–152. Lamb #2: Mohair and wool-blend yarn by www.misshawklet.com.

Lemur: Lion brand Wool-Ease Worsted in Gray Heather #620–151, Black #620–153, and Fisherman #620–099.

Lion: Lion brand Wool-Ease Worsted in Fuchsia #620–137 and Buttercup #620–158.

Mouse: Lion brand Wool-Ease Worsted in Azalea Pink #620–195, Oxford Gray #620–152, Fisherman #620–099, and Black #620–153.

Octopus: Lion brand Wool-Ease Worsted in Fisherman #620–099.

Owl: Lion brand Wool-Ease Worsted in Gold #620–171, Azalea Pink #620–195, and Avocado #620–174.

Penguin: Lion brand Wool-Ease Worsted in Gray Heather #620–151, Black #620–153, and Fisherman #620–099.

Pig: Lion brand Wool-Ease Worsted in Rose Heather 620–140.

Pup: Lion brand Wool-Ease Worsted in Avocado #620–174 and Lilac #620–146.

Turtle: TLC Essentials Yarn in Winter White #2316, Light Country Rose #2772, Robin Egg #2820, and Cranberry #2915.

Index